Ecosystems Research Journal

Serengeti
Research Journal

Natalie Hyde

CRABTREE
PUBLISHING COMPANY
WWW.CRABTREEBOOKS.COM

CRABTREE
PUBLISHING COMPANY
WWW.CRABTREEBOOKS.COM

Author: Natalie Hyde

Editors: Sonya Newland, Kathy Middleton

Design: Clare Nicholas

Cover design: Abigail Smith

Illustrator: Ron Dixon

Proofreader: Wendy Scavuzzo

**Production coordinator and
  prepress technician:** Tammy McGarr

Print coordinator: Katharine Berti

Produced for Crabtree Publishing Company
by White-Thomson Publishing

Photo Credits:

Cover: All images from Shutterstock

Interior: Alamy: p. 16r Steve Taylor ARPS; iStock: pp. 10–11 brytta, p. 11b Kenneth Canning, p. 14t ilbusca, p. 14b Jannie_nikola, p. 28 irvingnsaperstein; Getty Images: p.27b Martin Harvey; Shutterstock: pp. 4–5 Angela N Perryman, p. 5l Eric Isselee, p. 6l Four Oaks, p. 6r Gerrit_de_Vries, p. 7t Eric Isselee, p. 7b Bildagentur Zoonar GmbH, p. 8t Nickolay Stanev, p. 8b Aleksandr Sadkov, p. 9t Nick Fox, p. 9b Stuart G Porter, p. 10b Hein Nouwens, p. 11t Abdelrahman Hassanein, p. 12t EcoPrint, pp. 12–13 MattiaATH, p. 15 Harry S. Photos, p. 16l wolffpower, p. 17t Dietmar Temps, pp. 18–19 Eric Isselee, p. 18b GTS Productions, p. 19t Hein Nouwens, p. 19b Erwin Niemand, p. 20l Liz O'Neill, p. 20r Dr Ajay Kumar Singh, p. 21t Gudkov Andrey, p. 21b Delbars, p. 22b Morphart Creation, pp. 22–23 Alex van Schaik, p.23t Magdalena Paluchowska, p. 23b gualtiero boffi, p. 24 Attila Jandi, pp. 24–25 GTS Productions, p.25 Gudkov Andrey, p. 26 Travel Stock, p. 27t Morphart Creation, p. 27m Pierre Jean Durieu, p. 29 Eric Isselee; Wikimedia: p. 17b Marie-Elisabeth Gorge.

Library and Archives Canada Cataloguing in Publication

Hyde, Natalie, 1963-, author
    Serengeti research journal / Natalie Hyde.

(Ecosystems research journal)
Includes index.
Issued in print and electronic formats.
ISBN 978-0-7787-4660-7 (hardcover).--
ISBN 978-0-7787-4673-7 (softcover).--
ISBN 978-1-4271-2064-9 (HTML)

    1. Serengeti Plain (Tanzania)--Juvenile literature. 2. Biotic communities--Tanzania--Serengeti Plain--Juvenile literature. 3. Ecology--Tanzania--Serengeti--Serengeti Plain--Juvenile literature. I. Title.

QH195.T3H93 2018   j577.409678   C2017-907621-3
                                                C2017-907622-1

Library of Congress Cataloging-in-Publication Data

CIP Available at the Library of Congress

Crabtree Publishing Company
www.crabtreebooks.com   1-800-387-7650

Printed in the U.S.A./022018/CG20171220

Published in Canada
Crabtree Publishing
616 Welland Ave.
St. Catharines, Ontario
L2M 5V6

Published in the United States
Crabtree Publishing
PMB 59051
350 Fifth Avenue, 59th Floor
New York, New York 10118

Published in the United Kingdom
Crabtree Publishing
Maritime House
Basin Road North, Hove
BN41 1WR

Published in Australia
Crabtree Publishing
3 Charles Street
Coburg North
VIC, 3058

Contents

Mission to the Serengeti   4

Field Journal Day 1: Southern Serengeti National Park   6

Field Journal Day 2: Ngorongoro Conservation Area   8

Field Journal Day 3: Moru Kopjes, Serengeti National Park   10

Field Journal Day 4: Seronera Area   12

Field Journal Day 5: Grumeti River   14

Field Journal Day 6: Singita Grumeti Reserves   16

Field Journal Day 7: Ikorongo Reserve   18

Field Journal Day 8: Mara River   20

Field Journal Day 9: Maasai Mara   22

Field Journal Day 10: Loliondo Game Controlled Area   24

Field Journal Day 11: Ngorongoro Crater   26

Final Report   28

Your Turn   30

Learning More   31

Glossary & Index   32

Mission to the Serengeti

The Great **Migration**. That is the name given to the movement of animals across the grasslands in Africa called the Serengeti. The Serengeti Wildlife Foundation wants a **zoologist** to follow the migration. I am thrilled to be picked! The migration is a year-round, ongoing cycle. I will start my investigation in the south. I'll see where the cycle begins in January, then follow the route to the west. After seeing where the herds spend the spring, I will head north to the Mara. I hope to catch up with the herds there. Then I will travel ahead of the migration to the east to see what challenges will be in store for them. Finally, I will head back to the south where I started. I am going to study what changes might be endangering the animals. I will also document programs that are helping to protect the balance of life in the Serengeti.

The Serengeti is a vast area of grassland in Africa.

Some of things I will watch for are:
- **climate change**
- increase in tourists
- **poaching**
- effects on **Indigenous** peoples
- protection of wildlife
- fires
- disease
- increasing human population

There is no winter in Africa. The Serengeti has only dry an[d wet]
seasons. The short, or lighter, rains are in November to Dec[ember].
The long, or heavier, rains are March to May. The herds circle the
plains, following the rains to find fresh grass and water. More
than one million wildebeest make this migration each year,
along with zebras, and antelopes such as elands and gazelles.
The Serengeti **ecosystem** includes national parks, game reserves,
and wildlife corridors across Tanzania and Kenya. The Serengeti
National Park in Tanzania was created in 1951.
It is huge: 5,695 square miles (14,750 square
kilometers). There are no towns or villages
inside the park borders. The only people who
live there are park staff, some scientists, and
staff who work at the **lodges** and hotels.

Mara River

Maasai Mara

KENYA

Ikorongo Reserve

Grumeti Reserve

Grumeti River

Loliondo Game Controlled Area

Great Migration

Seronera

Serengeti National Park

TANZANIA

Moru Kopjes

Ngorongoro Conservation Area

Maswa Game Reserve

Lake Ndutu

Ngorongoro Crater

Serengeti National Park

Other parts of the Serengeti

Field Journal: Day 1

Southern Serengeti National Park

I start in the southern plains of Serengeti National Park in Tanzania. This is where the herds are in January. There is plenty of short grass for the 400,000 Thompson's gazelles, 12,000 elands, 300,000 zebras, and about 1.2 million wildebeest that make up the migration herds. The Serengeti ecosystem has both woodlands and grasslands. The large numbers of grazing animals eat the **saplings** as well as the grass. This keeps trees from taking over the grasslands.

Wildebeest are not likely to die of old age. They are more likely to be eaten by lions, hyenas, or other **predators** along their route. ↓

↑ Grazing animals such as impalas help control the spread of trees.

Wildebeest

In the 1900s, an infectious disease called **rinderpest** killed off many wildebeest and gazelles. With fewer grazing animals to eat the saplings, the trees began to thrive. Grasslands turned to forest. The balance between wildlife and habitat changed. In 1950, a **vaccine** for rinderpest was developed. The disease is now officially gone from the area. The number of wildebeest rebounded quickly. They began eating saplings again. As I look out at the Serengeti, I can see that some large trees remain, but the landscape is mostly grassland. The ecosystem is back in balance.

natstat STATUS REPORT ST456/part B

Name: African wild dog (Lycaon pictus)

Description:
African wild dogs live in packs. They have red, brown, black, and white patches of fur. This helps them hide in the grass. Each animal has a different pattern. Packs often share food. They will hunt animals much larger than themselves as a group. They eat antelopes and even wildebeest. Sometimes, they will attack cattle on farms outside park boundaries. Farmers hunt them to protect their livestock.

Attach photograph here ➡

Threats:
Habitat loss, disease, hunting

Numbers:
Fewer than 5,000

Status:
Endangered

7

Young wildebeest are easy prey for lions and other predators.

Ngorongoro Conservation Area

The herds move south in February to the Ngorongoro Conservation Area. I drive to the Ngorongoro Crater, which is the remains of a volcano that erupted long ago. Now it is a lush grassland. Most wildebeest give birth here around this time. Around 500,000 calves are born within two or three weeks. Predators such as lions, cheetahs, and hyenas hover nearby. They will prey on the weak adults and newborns. This keeps the herd's numbers from becoming too large for the plains. It also helps keep the herd healthy.

Ol Doinyo Lengai volcano is one of the most unusual volcanoes here. Its lava is black instead of orange when it erupts. Minerals in the lava make the grasses very nutritious for wildebeest and their young.

Tourists look out across the Ngorongoro Conservation Area from a viewing point.

The Ngorongoro Conservation Area was created to protect wildlife from poaching and habitat loss. In 1959, **UNESCO** named it an International Biosphere Reserve. This means it is a unique ecosystem that deserves protection. Conservationists find ways to balance tourism with protecting the people and wildlife there. The money tourists bring in helps to pay for programs such as making wildlife corridors for the migration. The corridors are wide, grassy pathways that link two larger animal habitats. They guide the herds away from farms. Other programs study how many tourists and vehicles can visit without harming the environment.

natstat STATUS REPORT ST456/part B

Name: Serval (Leptailurus serval)

Description:
Servals are medium-sized cats. They live in areas with tall grasses or reeds. Their golden coats are spotted and striped to help them blend in with their surroundings. They prey on rats, small birds, reptiles, and frogs. Their strong sense of hearing helps them hunt. When they hear their prey, they jump up to 7 feet (2.1 meters) in the air and land on it.

Attach photograph here →

Threats:
Habitat loss, hunted for fur, killed by farmers to protect livestock

Numbers:
About 3,300 in the Ngorongoro Crater

Status:
Least concern (many are in protected reserves)

Field Journal: Day 3

Moru Kopjes, Serengeti National Park

In March, the herds have eaten most of the grass in the south. The migration starts to move again. I am heading northwest to the Moru Kopjes. A kopje is a small hill of granite. It rises up out of a flat area. Kopjes have their own ecosystems, with different plants than on the plains. There are also different animals, such as hyraxes, lizards, and mongooses. Trees take root in the cracks of the rocks, and provide shade. Predators climb the kopjes and use them as lookout points.

Kopje

Sightings

Last night, I spotted a klipspringer. This small antelope lives only on the kopjes, where it finds food at night.

Klipspringer

As I climbed the Moru Kopjes, I was excited to see a black rhino on the plain. This area is one of the last places they live in the wild. Black rhinos have been hunted almost to **extinction**. Farmers see them as a threat to their crops. Hunters want their horns. Africa loses about three rhinos per day. Some black rhinos were taken to a South African zoo, where they had young. These young rhinos were returned to the Serengeti. Radio transmitters were placed in their horns so they could be tracked. They are guarded around the clock by the Serengeti Rhino Protection Unit.

In some countries, ground-up rhino horn is thought to cure diseases.

natstat STATUS REPORT ST456/part B

Name: Rock hyrax (Procavia capensis)

Threats: Hunted for their meat and fur, diseases such as mange, considered pests by farmers, habitat loss

Description:

This little mammal looks like a large guinea pig or rabbit, but it is actually a relative of the elephant. Its teeth, toes, and skull are similar to those of an elephant. It even has two tiny teeth that grow out like tusks. The rubbery pads on its feet help it climb on the rocks of the kopjes. Rock hyraxes start their day sunbathing on the rocks. They will not even come out of their burrows if it is cool or rainy.

Numbers: Widespread

Status: Least concern

Attach photograph here ➡️

Field Journal: Day 4

Seronera Area

Our guide drives the jeep over the rough trail to the Seronera area. This is where most of the wildebeest had been around April. But we are surprised to find the open plains here are not covered with grass—everything is burned black. Our guide says the park rangers set fires every season after the migration passes through. If the herds get enough food just by eating grass, they don't always eat the young saplings. That means trees will start to grow. Setting fires clears the trees away, leaving only a few. It also leaves grass at different heights. This encourages a greater variety of wildlife.

The red grass called *Themeda triandra* can live through a fire. It is not as nutritious for wildebeest as other grasses. But sometimes it is all that is left after a **seasonal** fire.

Animals such as these impalas lick the ash to get minerals.

Bush fire

I spoke to one scientist studying the fire damage. She said some researchers believe that setting fires isn't necessary. They say there are enough grazing animals now to keep the forest from taking over the grasslands. They think that fires should only happen naturally, from sources such as lightning. She was writing a report comparing areas that had fires set with areas that were left to burn naturally. They are still waiting to see the long-term effects of both systems.

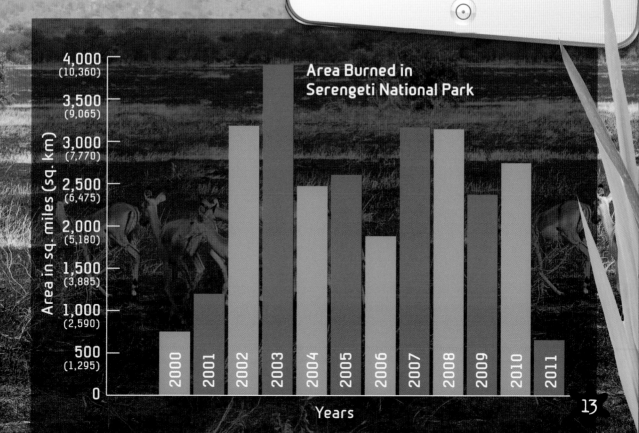

Area Burned in Serengeti National Park

Area in sq. miles (sq. km)	
4,000 (10,360)	
3,500 (9,065)	
3,000 (7,770)	
2,500 (6,475)	
2,000 (5,180)	
1,500 (3,885)	
1,000 (2,590)	
500 (1,295)	
0	

Years: 2000 2001 2002 2003 2004 2005 2006 2007 2008 2009 2010 2011

Grumeti River

We headed to the Grumeti River, where the herds crossed around May. I wondered why two different species, the wildebeest and zebras, traveled together. My guide told me that the two species work together. They don't compete for food. Zebras eat the tall tops of grass. Wildebeest eat short grass near the roots. Zebras have strong memories. They can remember migration routes and the best places to cross rivers such as the Grumeti. Wildebeest need to drink more often than zebras. They are excellent at finding water sources even when the plains look dry. This is very important in years of severe **drought**.

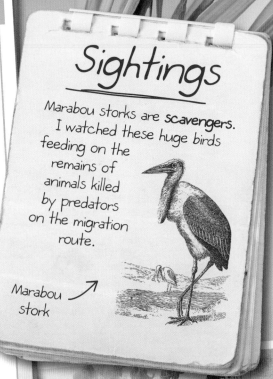

Sightings

Marabou storks are **scavengers**. I watched these huge birds feeding on the remains of animals killed by predators on the migration route.

Marabou stork ↗

Predators and drowning make each river crossing a risk for the animals.

14

Lions help keep the numbers of grazing animals in balance in the Serengeti. In 1994, a disease called **canine distemper** spread to lions from dogs that live with humans. The disease affects the major organs and there is no known cure. It killed 30 percent of the Serengeti lions that year. At first, it spread only from dogs to lions. Biologists I spoke to told me that they now think it can spread from lion to lion. It also infects hyenas, jackals, and foxes. This shows one of the ways in which wild ecosystems such as the Serengeti are affected by humans living close by.

Lions are one of the top predators in this ecosystem.

Years of Severe Drought in the Serengeti

1966
3 years

1969
4 years

number of years between droughts

1973
20 years

1993
1 year

1994
1 year

1995
11 years

2006
3 years

2009
4 years

2013
4 years

2017

Field Journal: Day 6

Baboons and other monkeys can be seen in the Singita Grumeti Reserves.

Beehive fence

I saw crops being protected by beehives hanging from wires. The bees will come out and scare off elephants or other animals if they touch this beehive fence.

Singita Grumeti Reserves

Today I traveled to the Singita Grumeti Reserves. The herds make their way here by June. This area lies outside the national park. At one time, this space was used as private hunting land. It was divided into three **hunting concessions**. Animals were not protected. The concession owners came together in 2002 to create a wildlife corridor for the migration. No hunting is allowed in the corridors. Anti-poaching teams help to protect endangered species. Animal populations in the area are healthy and growing.

The Reserves are also the site of the Grumeti Horticultural and Marketing **Co-op** Society (GHOMACOS). This is a gardening and market co-op for local farmers. They supply lodges in the area with high-quality, locally grown food. This benefits farmers with small farms. It also means that local people can earn money by providing food for tourists and reserves. As a result they are less likely to poach animals to sell for money or to eat themselves. They are also more likely to be interested in conservation of the area if their living is based on it.

↑ This woman has grown bananas to sell.

natstat STATUS REPORT ST456/part B

Name: Mpingo tree (Dalbergia melanoxylon)

Description:
This small tree is a slow grower. It is not large enough to be harvested until it is 70–100 years old. It has dense, black wood. It is in demand for making musical instruments such as clarinets and oboes. Between 7,500 and 20,000 mpingo trees are cut down each year. But the twisted trunk and branches mean only small sections can be used for carving. Around 90 percent of the cut tree is wasted.

Attach photograph here

Threats:
Illegal logging, over-harvesting

Numbers:
3 million

Status:
Near-threatened in the Serengeti

17

Field Journal: Day 7

Rain over the Serengeti

Ikorongo Reserve

By July, the migration has usually moved to the Ikorongo Reserve. This area was created to continue the protected corridor to the northern Serengeti. I drove with a local guide to inspect the grasslands. He told me that they had very little rain this year. The grass had not grown very much. This meant the migration probably wouldn't stay in this area very long. The animals would keep moving north to find more food. He reminded me that the migration is not a perfect circle. The direction depends a lot on the rains. If there is plenty, the herds will stay longer in one area. If it is dry, they may move farther east or west to find food.

If grass is scarce, elands and other animals will move on quickly.

Sightings

I spotted a black-and-white colobus monkey in an acacia tree. They spread seeds with their sloppy eating.

← Colobus monkey

Climate change has affected the seasons here. Climate change is in climate patterns all over the w to the warming of Earth's tempera Weather conditions can become ex and lead to dangerous droughts or flooding. In Africa, lack of rain is becoming a big problem. Dry plains with no fresh grass will affect migration routes and the health of the herds. On the other hand, plenty of rain means that plenty of food will grow. The animals will have no need to migrate. Predators in other regions need food to survive, too. If the herds come late or not at all, many predators along the migration route will die.

natstat STATUS REPORT ST456/part B

Name: Secretary bird (Sagittarius serpentarius)

Description:
This large bird of prey has long legs and a bill like an eagle. It hunts mostly on the ground, eating mice, snakes, crabs, and lizards. These birds stomp their prey until it is dead. Secretary birds build their nests high in acacia trees. The pale-green eggs hatch after 45 days.

Threats:
Deforestation, habitat loss, flying into power lines

Numbers:
Fewer than 65,000

Status:
Vulnerable

Attach photograph here →

Mara River

This is the most exciting day! I will catch up with the migrating herds in the northern Serengeti National Park. It is on the border with Kenya. I am heading to the most famous crossing on the Mara River. Tens of thousands of wildebeest make their way down the slopes of the steep cliffs here to the banks of the river. The water level of the river is becoming more irregular from year to year. Some years, it is almost dry. There have been heavy rains here this year. The water is high in the river. Animals may drown if they cannot scramble up the slippery **exit banks** on the other side. They may also be taken by predators including lions, crocodiles, and hyenas, which wait along the shore.

Over half the deaths on the migration route are from disease or injuries. Scavengers eat the bodies. Hyenas and vultures depend on this food source.

Tourists waiting to watch the crossing

There were many rules for tourists watching the herd crossing. We were not allowed to get too close before the herds began to move. Once they started crossing, we could move to a good location for pictures. But we were not allowed to get out of our jeeps. It is too dangerous with all the predators around. The Mara River is famous for its huge Nile crocodiles. Getting too close could also spook the herds. They might head in the wrong direction and drown. Park rangers stayed nearby. They would fine anyone interfering with the migration.

natstat STATUS REPORT ST456/part B

Name: Cheetah (Acinonyx jubatus)

Threats:
Habitat loss, hunting

Numbers: 9,000–12,000

Description:
The cheetah is the fastest mammal on land. It can run up to 68 miles (110 km) per hour. After a chase, a cheetah needs time to catch its breath. It has to wait about half an hour before it can eat. It eats small- to medium-sized animals such as hares, impalas, gazelles, and baby wildebeest.

Status:
Vulnerable in the Serengeti region; critically endangered in North and West Africa

Attach photograph here ➡

In the language of the Maasai, Serengeti means "endless plains."

Maasai Mara

I decide to head farther into the Maasai Mara, a national reserve in Kenya. The Mara is the traditional land of the Maasai. They are an Indigenous people from the area. In the past, they moved from place to place with their livestock in search of fresh grass. Land to graze their cattle is decreasing. Lately, more Maasai are staying in one place. They are adding to their diet by farming vegetables such as corn and beans.

Sightings

The prickly pear cactus is not native to the Serengeti. It was brought to the area as a plant for lodge gardens. It is an **invasive species** that is taking over sensitive grasslands.

Prickly pear cactus →

The Maasai graze their cattle on the grasslands of the Serengeti.

The Mara Reserve is important to both the migrating herds and the Maasai people. The area has the only **salt licks** for animals. However, the reserve's fences stop the Maasai's cattle from reaching them. In dry seasons, most of the available water is also inside the reserve. This causes a conflict between the needs of the reserve and the Maasai people. Fortunately, there are organizations working to help fix this conflict. The Mara Naboisho Conservancy works to balance the needs of the migrating animals, Maasai people, and tourists.

natstat STATUS REPORT ST456/part B

Name: Spotted hyena
(Crocuta crocuta)

Threats:
Habitat loss

Description:
Spotted hyenas are also called "laughing hyenas." They live in clans with up to 100 members. They can make eleven different sounds with their voices. When they are nervous, they giggle like a human laugh. They also grunt, growl, groan, and squeak. Lions and hyenas compete for the same food. Hyenas may plan and hunt for hours only to have their catch stolen by a lion.

Numbers: 27,000–47,000

Status:
Least concern, but the population is decreasing

Attach photograph here ➡

23

Field Journal: Day 10

Loliondo Game Controlled Area

Today, I traveled back across the border into Tanzania to the Loliondo Game Controlled Area. This is another concession that was created to protect the migration. I joined the Tanzania Wildlife Conservation Monitoring team there. The TWCM is a program that was formed in 1989. It tracks wildlife numbers and observes habitats in Tanzania's protected areas. I am joining the team on an **aerial survey** to observe the area where the herds will arrive in October and November.

From the air, we took photos of the parks, lodges, and roads.

There have already been big benefits to **monitoring**. One of the most important was discovering that severe poaching of the cape buffalo was taking place. Park rangers used the information to try to save the remaining buffalo.

Cape buffalo do not migrate.

Population of Wildebeest

Year	Population
1957	250,000
1960	300,000
1965	400,000
1970	650,000
1975	1.4 million
1980	1.35 million
1985	1.2 million
1990	1.25 million
1995	850,000
2000	1.2 million

From above, we will be able to see where safari vehicles are travelling off the the roads. This damages the fragile ecosystem. On our flight, we can spot where farmers are creating new fields illegally in restricted areas. The information we gather will help the TWCM team to preserve and protect this area. It will show where better law enforcement is needed. It will also show how wildlife is affected by activities outside protected areas, such as building fences around crops or livestock. They will be able to create maps for special purposes. Some will reveal where there are vehicle tracks in the Ngorongoro Crater. We can also see where towns and villages are growing. This leads to more contact between humans and wildlife.

A herd of blue wildebeest

Field Journal: Day 11

Beautiful flamingos were feeding along the shores of Lake Ndutu. This lake is in the center of the Ngorongoro Crater.

Ngorongoro Crater

I have traveled back to the Ngorongoro Conservation Area. I am staying in a mobile tent camp. The hotel staff told me that tourism in the Serengeti is at an all-time high. Close to 2 million travelers visit the area each year. Tourism has good and bad effects. It creates jobs for local people in hotels and on safaris. The money from tourism helps support conservation and education projects. Roads, airports, and lodges have been built. But trucks and safari jeeps wear away grass cover. Noise and pollution can disturb animals and natural habitats. The extra water needed for tourists and lodges can affect the water available for plants, animals, and local people.

I have come full circle on my migration journey. By December, the zebras, wildebeest, and gazelles will come back here where they started. The rains will come just as they arrive, and bring the grasslands back to life. The herds will stay here for about two months. By then, all the grass will be eaten. Then the herds will be on the move again.

Sightings

The lake is a great place to watch water birds, such as ibises and saddle-bill storks.

Ibis

Mobile tent camp
↓

natstat STATUS REPORT ST456/part B

Name: Southern African hedgehog
(*Atelerix frontalis*)

Threats:
Habitat loss, killed by vehicles, hunted for food, used as medicine

Description:
The body of this little mammal is covered with sharp spines. When it is threatened, it curls into a ball with its spikes outward. It eats mainly insects such as crickets and earthworms. It lives in holes in the ground covered by bushes or leaves. Females usually have four young at a time.

Numbers: Widespread

Status:
Least concern, but numbers are decreasing

Attach photograph here ➡

Final Report

REPORT TO:
SERENGETI WILDLIFE FOUNDATION

OBSERVATIONS

The search for food drives the greatest migration on Earth. The herds of the Serengeti follow the rains that bring fresh grass to dry ground. Anything that changes the rain pattern threatens the health of the ecosystem. Fires and diseases are a natural part of the ecosystem. But closer contact with towns and tourists can wipe out entire herds. Rules are important to protect both the wildlife and visitors.

FUTURE CONCERNS

Climate change is affecting the rain patterns in the Serengeti. Long dry spells mean grass cannot grow. The herds could face starvation. Heavy rains can make river crossings deadly. They can also make the herds stay in one area longer than normal. Predators and scavengers in other areas will be affected. Changing rain patterns also make it difficult for Indigenous peoples to farm. They will often turn to poaching to survive. This puts endangered animals at a greater risk.

CONSERVATION PROJECTS

Tourism brings in much-needed money. The national parks and reserves use the money to employ park rangers and support programs such as the Serengeti Rhino Protection Unit. Tourism also provides a living for local people, who provide goods through co-op programs such a GHOMACOS. But it is also important to balance the number of visitors with the needs of wildlife and Indigenous peoples. Careful monitoring is helpful. It can show where changes need to be made in the number or location of lodges and trails. With careful controls and respect for all the life in the Serengeti region, it is hoped the Great Migration will continue as it has done for millions of years.

Your Turn

✱ Look at the chart of severe drought years in the Serengeti on page 15. One of those years was 2017. Find out more about how the drought affected people and animals in the Serengeti in 2017. Using your research and the information in this book, write a short report on the effects of a lack of rain in the region.

✱ Many areas of the Serengeti National Park use controlled fires to kill off tree saplings. They say it is important to stop the trees from taking over the grasslands. What might happen if more of the grasslands turn to forest?

✱ More and more people want to witness the Great Migration. More tourists mean more roads through the park, more lodges, and more waste. What are some new ways that the national parks can protect the ecosystem, while still allowing people to marvel at the migration?

Learning More

BOOKS

Chasing Cheetahs: The Race to Save Africa's Fastest Cat by Sy Montgomery (HMH Books for Young Readers, 2014)

National Geographic Readers: Lions by Laura Marsh (National Geographic Children's Books, 2015)

The Great Migration by Deborah Lock (DK Children, 2012)

WEBSITES

http://video.nationalgeographic.com/video/wildebeest_migration
This video by National Geographic shows the huge herds of wildebeest and zebras on the move.

http://kids.nationalgeographic.com/explore/secret-life-of-the-serengeti/
If you want to know how many different animals visit a water hole in the Serengeti, this website will show you.

http://justfunfacts.com/interesting-facts-about-serengeti-national-park/
Incredible photos illustrate interesting facts about Serengeti National Park.

Glossary & Index

aerial survey   gathering information about the land from a plane

canine distemper   a virus with no cure, which causes breathing and digestive system problems

climate change   a change in weather patterns in a particular area over a long period of time

co-op   a group of people working together in a business or organization

drought   a long period when there is no rain

ecosystem   a community of living things and their environment

endangered   at risk of becoming extinct

exit banks   slopes down to the water to make an easy exit for animals crossing it

extinction   when there are no more living members of a species

hunting concessions   land where certain people have the right to hunt

Indigenous   native to a place

invasive species   plants or animals not native to an area, which spread easily

lodges   hotels in a national park or game reserve

migration   when animals move from one area to another

monitoring   watching over and reporting on something

poaching   hunting animals without permission

predators   animals that hunt other animals

rinderpest   an infectious disease that usually causes death

salt licks   places where animals go to lick salt from the ground

saplings   young trees

scavengers   animals that feed on dead animals

seasonal   happening at a certain time each year

UNESCO   the United Nations Educational, Scientific and Cultural Organization; it helps run programs in education, science, and the arts

vaccine   a substance that stops the spread of disease

zoologist   a scientist who studies animals

African wild dogs 7

beehives 16
black rhinos 11

canine distemper 15
cape buffalo 24
cheetahs 8, 21
climate change 4, 19, 29
conservation programs 9, 11, 17, 23, 24, 25, 26, 29
crocodiles 20, 21

disease 4, 6, 7, 11, 15, 20, 28
droughts 14, 15, 19

elands 5, 6, 18

farms and farmers 7, 9, 11, 17, 22, 25, 29
fires 4, 12, 13, 28

gazelles 5, 6, 7, 21, 27
GHOMACOS 17, 29
grasses 5, 6, 8, 9, 10, 12, 13, 14, 18, 19, 22, 27, 28, 29
Grumeti Reserves 5, 16, 17
Grumeti River 5, 14

habitat loss 7, 9, 11, 19, 21, 23, 27
hunting 7, 9, 11, 16, 21, 27
hyenas 6, 8, 15, 20, 23

Ikorongo Reserve 18
impalas 6, 12, 21

Indigenous peoples 4, 22, 23, 29
invasive species 22

Kenya 5, 20, 22
klipspringers 10
kopjes 10, 11

Lake Ndutu 26, 27
lions 6, 8, 15, 20, 23
livestock 7, 9, 22, 25
Loliondo Game Controlled Area 24

Maasai Mara 4, 5, 22
Maasai people 22, 23
Mara Naboisho Conservancy 23
Mara River 5, 20, 21
marabou storks 14
mongooses 10

monitoring 24, 29
monkeys 16, 19
mpingo trees 17

Ngorongoro Conservation Area 8, 9, 26
Ngorongoro Crater 8, 9, 25, 26

Ol Doinyo Lengai 8

poaching 4, 9, 16, 17, 24
prickly pear 22

rain 5, 18, 20, 28, 29
rinderpest 7
rock hyraxes 10, 11

secretary birds 19

Serengeti National Park 5, 6, 20
Serengeti Rhino Protection Unit 11, 29
southern African hedgehog 27

Tanzania 5, 6, 24
tourism 4, 9, 17, 20, 21, 23, 26, 28, 29
trees 6, 7, 10, 12, 17, 19
TWCM 24, 25

water 5, 23, 26
wildebeest 5, 6, 7, 8, 12, 14, 20, 21, 25, 27
wildlife corridors 5, 9, 16, 18

zebras 5, 6, 14, 27